The
Nerve
Epistle

The
Nerve
Epistle

Sarah Riggs

ROOF BOOKS
NEW YORK

ISBN: 978-1-7379703-0-9
Library of Congress Control Number: 2021946750

Cover art by Sarah Riggs
Author photograph by Omar Berrada
Frontis photograph © Hillary Goidell

"Dear Ashraf" and "Dear Etel" appear in *The Poetry Project*, in November 2018, online. "Dear Rachel Levitsky," "Dear Hillary Goidell," and "Dear Liliane Giraudon" appeared in *New American Writing 39*. "Dear Emily Wallis Hughes" appeared in Hughes' book of poetry, *Sugar Factory*, Spuyten Duyvil, 2019, with Sarah Riggs' paintings. "Dear Basel Ghattas" appeared, in an Arabic translation by Safaa Fathy, in *Doha Magazine*, issue 144, October 2019. Celina Su and Sarah Riggs' correspondence appeared in *The Brooklyn Rail*, summer 2021. "Anne Waldman" and "Dear Janice Lowe" appeared in Visible Binary, 2021, online.

NEW YORK STATE OF OPPORTUNITY | Council on the Arts   This book is made possible, in part, by the New York State Council on the Arts with the support of Governor Andrew Cuomo and the New York State Legislature.

Roof Books
are published by
Segue Foundation
300 Bowery, New York, NY 10012
seguefoundation.com

Roof Books
are distributed by
Small Press Distribution
1341 Seventh Street
Berkeley, CA. 94710-1403
800-869-7553 or spdbooks.org

Contents

7/15/17

Dear Safaa,

I saw the wind reach through
your ears again, and you made a huge
smile in words, flashing through your
teeth. It was the unseasoned hour
of breathing fish and our gills were
choked with massacre, the rain along
the avenues coming out red.
We were getting younger in our palms
turned and curled in through these
mornings or night hours, it was
said so, fleeting and winded, you in
the sun for a second, having
to come out blue, and the verdant
decorations all we could think of
subtly to that mark. Some
kind of wound held together by
separation. Never to know the end
of it, transitioning back to the
inner thoughts made up of
dominoes and concrete leaves.
Several thousand people had
fit into that square thinking
it was a circle of souls.
The bodies separated out
and we were left with maps and
archives, some branches, and
ancient intuitions. These lines
weave through yours, and the
thinking goes around, far into
where we will be.

Jenny:

The ocean and the sea
switching places and while I have
you on the phone, please send waves
and a chronic of the trees, some tales
of rain & a compendium of stars
so we can retain the wisdom of
our errors, fill in the middle
of the songs with a moon, the
one on Thursday nights, slightly
pink and marbled, in a hat of
a thousand and one ribbons such
we met together over the bittersweet
face of words become music, tamed
in the hour of distress mingled with
joy, there in a song, yours
tales out of season—
The rain does round this moon
and the winds come through the waves
we can't believe the skies
however the world turns we're on it

Dear Layla May,

The quickening of the tides in your
hair and that discovery, told now, into
the breech, and you learning a word
letting down the senses, acid along
the sides of the tongue further back
a history of tasting, direct and
determined, the sycamore poised
on the edge of autumn, more or
less, to an inch close from home
a telling more than an ounce, or
seventeen eleven, such a quick dose
of it present, told, or remaindered

Dear François,

The lick of the orange is bead.
The tenor of the boat is fleck.
The range of the water is shell.
The determined of the minute is hand.
The flower of the sandle is vein.
The tendency of the doubt is tame.
The challenge of the object is green.
The tease of the harmony is hung.
The tick of the wither is tame.
The winter of statue is vote.
The terrain of the second is weather.

Sarita,

The swallows' thirst comes in with
The yellow grasses and we are seated
And waiting, hollow in that sound
A triangular whispering, and the
monks are wandering outside the walls
we are waiting for the answer and the
answer is green

You are in your mourning
clothes and there's a rippling of desire over
the highway not so very old or particularly
young we were keen to get back and
the grasses were going that way
turbid and sure in that hour of
maybe's, there were sores in the
world growing into wounds and the
wounds festering and the media feeding
there and you had to get back
though it was good to be away for sure
as the evening creeps in in grasses

Cole:

The attention given to dots and lines
A furthering along the measure of flat
You hoisted the telling genre
Fishing futile in this case
Remarkable teased to the ground
What it was the increased time
We wanted that, and that too
Some renditions of time waxing
And of your thoughts waning
Miserable conditions and the process of witness
A woman came up to us and began to speak
Of the Arkansas 8 and how trauma revisits with age
A cascading at that point of angled tales, steps

Cole's response:

Remarkable Along

Some rendition of witness
will, within the waxing,
will, within the wanting,
will measure it on down—

—increased ground—

We wanted that waxing;
we wanted that telling, that too
 increased time,
and time, in its furthering,
began, in its speaking,
revisiting our thoughts;
our thoughts came back to us
angled in increased attention,
increasing, too, age and point and cascading point.

Dear Ashraf,

I heard you were there
not being able to imagine it
we are writing you this song
how to send love to someone
never met. Heard you there.
Habib imprisoned this week.
In or out. A penetrating
Dialogue. A wish to send
owl's wings. Caught and
imported. For that hour
second you there. Between
the films, sliver of an eye.
Sent you a rope to pull you
back into this place

Liliane:

Watering the plants you come to mind
oasis of swallows across landscape
you hollowed out into that slacking
credible place for sleep the two of you
and for that instance: certain
what came and went in the tree
you were mobile so flexible
for more, a thousand books flying
from one word, and the ongoing stories
keeping the women alive, though
a slight disapproving crease to the
mouth, how could you keep it
you assuredly in a crevice below
a faint, nearly full moon so it
continues this way and we follow

Ana,

The cat call of place is winded.
The thick of buds is catch. The shake
of impression is metal. The hair of
water is glazed. The curtain of terror
is president. The small of tremor is
name. The double lane of cell is twain.
The match of ink is turbid.
The twitch of beads is luck. The
witch of disaster is you. The
remembering of before is birth.
The shake of lanes is candescent.
The vote of minorities is stacked against.
The sand of tea is clouds. The crack
of skull is before you.

Dad,

         We returned to
the undercurrents of language
with breakfast radiators.
Qualitatively diving into time
quenching retorts and rebuffs.
So it would be peppermint you
delaying the sun back shaft fall.
Or further along the alley two-day
growth and eighty-four you here.
The thickening into plants and cowering
shells of a thousand and two
varieties. Crept into distinct
blue architectures of a sudden
and forever carapace. A head of
crackling in the fierce grasses
this one you say easel. Retort
of remaining escalating spoons
in the clever dash angular.
Trot and feed so too query
at the copse said piece
along stuffed plainly. Talented
enamel and wishing slender
for ferocious camping the
hearts piled up in the rain.
Weary collective coming at
oblong decision tell the concerned
parrot to idle along. Quickly
went the fox tower treble
and ebony stronghold. Dominant
maneuver so thickly through
fire bright buffalo

April

Dear Hillary,

The pocket of regret pulled through
into a rainbow beam so suddenly
that we backed into each telling
with touching regard for some futures
long past told into the remainder
crying or so extended to each twist
formerly a keen shrug of underweather
bonding such we could say outright
into the collection fraught finding
the way around they say holding
on in a diminishment of quirky
gamesaying disaster in forewarning
getting large boots into that suckling
extended moment predisposed towards
tender and the shelling out
variety F just so frequent way
to sift the engines to lather
the fringes cutting equally in planes
of motion to that degree of finesse
wrought chainwalling bending in
a fury waxing along snail body
and jellyfish there a kind of thunder
very visceral and you would like
her so in that planet reversal in
which trees sunder on their leaves
paradoxically you bent forwards
along the taxi lines more or more
frowning upon the cuttings and
plastering made into sequels of tenacious
bluffing and calling wondrous oh you

To Robert Burns

I found a little mouse, deceased
next to the video projector in Paris.
I thought of you and how prescient
you were about human dominion.
I showed the girls who were
very curious indeed, there in a
little plastic bag as I was taking
it to the garbage. How human dominion
is certainly winning, breaking the
social union. How we are all destined
to go up to the sky, or into the
earth. Rocking the boat
raising the seas.

Dear Fred Tcheng,

The tint of the skeleton is violet.
The mild of the knowing is veined.
The wary of the time is rouge.
The cusp of the lies are turbid.
The angle of the look is dart.
The feature of the sky is soot.
The terror of the unknown is calm.
The mane of the sea is dry.
The stars of the cavern are newspaper.
The gun of the mass is smoke.
The tune of blue is green.
The frame of work is more.
The fringe of the hour is shaved.

Gail Scott:

The thought of you Gail trains
behind and ahead, a head full
of streamers. Stop the giving
tree says Julie and so
I try. There is a scarf of
loneliness along your shoulders
there, not eating an artichoke.
We pretend to remain in
the moment floating like Vera's
grandmother in something
that is not really the present, nor
the past or future either. The
waves make beaches in your
eyes. Today I tried to write to
Ashraf again.

Sister,

The sliced oval of melon
rinds in the light, caged hour
so many hermit crabs reaching
some sort of supremacy vomit
in Virginia
—the water has
magnetic pull
the sky will pull us away
(where she has gone)
the clawed antler of the female
fecund, deviant, searching through
something invested in the q
shorn of remembering, the
whipped present yielding
a sovereign leaf & misshapen
the toes on their sleeve and
a heart threaded floorwise
intensifying song quid pro
cohabitation in one room
so knowing sex in that beat
exuberance she has it quacking
or a rendition of crackling
the newspapers damp with lines
a hurtling obnoxious solar knob
horizons with fake ridges and breasts
into that rhododendron hour

July 20

Dear Michael,

Were to the ache: an assemblage
Lanes to the mild: a frozen remainder
Crumbling along spokes: flavor of unending
Multiple quixotic: zany queries
Falling along: we to the how
Some statements into mild: forgotten letters
Quick of split seconds: marked answers
Zest for cubes: angles leaving thought
Merely a vote: so to determinacy
I asked you: synesthesia of yes
The making of endings: blue blur new

Rachel,

       Place call now
generative, conversation inch
obedient, a tale of a cucumber
peppered, sail of laughter
caught, fervent impulses on trial
remainder of time tumult
supremacists sure of extreme
left hour jumped into right
quizzical determined
topical mingled, rind
softened in quick, thoroughly
zipped into relay, consensual
needing repeat, quickened to
leaf, wax of lane long
bannon is out, weather
pushing toward sides, kangaroos
ready & eating, twist of the
plastic out, fierce of the time
second, front of film down
sail of skin mixed
weight of time losing
freeze of ring hole, top
of Q trained, quick of
thing turbid, sure of wet
idea, body of color red
twirl of cloud lined, pace
of the bracelet broken

Sharifa Rhodes-Pitts:

The turning in events, protocol not reinvented
huge structures cycling, the absence of envy
and an emotional bargain through to rivers
timely and returned, your thesis of the Civil War
never-having-ended finds us on a bus, children
playing, and a tremendous venture in speculation
a thought process, nudged in particular ways
the massive thing of prison, the splotches of
population on the map in Brooklyn

the day after

Dear John Ashbery,

There are ears in the wind
can you see where you are, fleeting
but sunny, how we wish you were
here, so to go under, in the fraught
times with you here, with you there
move to an island of mirth, caught
there in your hair, tea and beer
so the telling of the wave
adventure and cautionary tales
such timber voice contented in
difficulty tear through it so to
say foretelling modesty crew time
a group of hands and moving pens
taught to waver and forbear
you too there, a terrific forerunner
through that thatch and mountain
sure sighting, carefully maneuvered
caught up in angle, the marooned
opinions of a cluster, why we
speak in off-tones, determined about
it or about nothing precisely
querulous tufted, into the wound
such to tell, frightened mixed
tones, desire hour set back, and
to ask now, demanding

Dear Rosmarie,

The time falls through the hours
and I am in love again, a porthole
in a very thick wall through which
wind is whistling. I could reach
your hand even your wrist and we
were whispering through our fingers
places we had heard in slips of
seconds. You wearing the scarf with
the colored shapes and I behind you
wearing the scarf with the colored shapes.
It was love or it was death, the two intertwined
and passing through the ears and between
mouths, you going first we thought
but then there were loved ones, younger
than you, who went first. A sense of not
being ready, being made beautiful by
Julie Patton, turning into a being ready.
You have your hands on my shoulders.
Rosmarie, guiding me between the
voices, and you laughing because it is
so funny, being alive at all.

Rosmarie's reply:

Dear Sarah,
hours whistle through our fingers
through the night
the scarf the same scarf
the two and passing through
the hidden differences of language
and between, we thought, but then we were
if we began thinking, not ready not
thinking with our heart
stammering sounds into the world
not tall our tales, finally
not between
just being alive

Love,
Rosmarie

Dear Julie,

You had us wrapped though the
inner ear of birth, of death. We were
passing through your arms your mouths
your words the middle passage you
said trump many times and black many
times you were spinning words saying
ask the children what they think you
had wrapped an orange turban around
your head you were wearing an orange
tunic with many spangled jewels

Dear Sharifa,

Some souls crying on a letter
you wished back, and the neighbor's
morning glories, till the 45th time
the arrangements in them bewildering
some superstorms and the world
watching, hovering, nightmares
and daymares, and we hardly able
to move, you are in Harlem
you are in Haiti, you are side-stepping
through Brooklyn, you are deep-stepping
through history, where are we going
who to heal the wounds. We are dropping
petals not bombs, we are holding
hands not clenching fists, we are
writing the waters rising, the tensions
extreme, we are here, we are
present, we are engaged, we will
not give in except when time takes us away

Martin,

There, as in here, there
and the quiet infused it, the shooting
of the minute, and we along a sunset
the poem was lying down, arms outstretched
wishing for sleep amid crisis, and our hands
were answering phones without bringing
them to the lips or ears, there was swearing
in the breathing of the nostrils
I had brought you a dangling
of morning glories along a rowboat
perched on a reflecting river you perhaps painted.
We entered the ears together for a moment
and it was a peaceful cacophony.
It is a long evening and I smile
as you turn to me and say
"What environmental crisis?" And
we in the wit laughing there
for a few minutes until the minutes
are gone

Martin's answer:

S.

Every summer river seems to be
in need of a reflection, whether
carried on its surface or on us.
Underneath the clouds there is
a mulchy bed of leaves and then perhaps
some morning glories or bindweed
precious for their transience
which we mime, wafting arms up at the sky
as insects mimic an alarm
the sky-blue boat sits moored
just for the moment
crisis dripped in amber light
if I remember clearly
when the image floated up before us
reminiscent of a vision
bringing us both here.

M.

p.s. An accusation often aimed at Art is that it represents a withdrawal from "real life." I can't see how a life exists without the mindful interaction such as Art allows, or how "real" a life can be without this interactive knowledge of itself.
p.p.s. Crises are not made by artists stepping out of our reality, crises are a sudden psychological eruption of awareness of the mindless catastrophic actions that an unreflecting "real life" has ignored.

Anne:

The persuasion of a silk scarf
under the moment. You say anthropocene
to the ears to the eyes through the voice
and we dwell in currents and indeterminacy.
Arms and gesture as one place where
we go to lodge, tertiary thoughts
and the trumpeting of articulation.
CAW CAW Janice Lowe makes
magic voice sounds and we are
in there, not just a word, the
way it gets said *anthropocene*
and a terrifying tremor to the very earth
suspended by your gesture
and one thing is sure is this
love that you exude, into the
hour, the lost world at least loved
and extending out and through
the mouth of the saxophone says
you-we-I and there's a gifting
of cedar, parts of the earth,
community dwelling and a treehouse
where we go, holding out hands
for each other.

Anne's response:

Sarah, the humanity...you and ,,,

"ek-stasis is the gift that singularity gathers from the empty hands of humanity"

Agamben

Your halo is rich perfect glow
and edges that are poems speak
that we think together in this night
an act in being night, telepathy across fields
O my mistress of tablet and paint
you are almost metaphysical
I think of cloth and daughter oud, of what
to risk and try and sound and trust
In Arab tradition agent intellect is Qlam, Pen
a potentiality, writing as you do of frames
of lost world and voice and indeterminacy
tremor, gesture back at you, sister *intellectus,*
how much you have changed and charged
my world, what is remedy but care
adopted to make weave, to translate
countries where one genuflects
reaches toward a more sublime synchronicity
like this when instruments talk
We don't want our bodies commodified
tree house for the rescue mission for
where we'll dwell when we are Tree
we are the matrix the mothers, allure
everything not touched by hand of cruel men
and I mean the world is our Nirvana
don't lose it but let it loose, carry
freedom in eye-storm this time we're here
to witness our companeras we'll fight for them
new eye opens newly to determine activity

with us help lead, modest we'll fight for
all our linguistic nature, *thyrathen*, being called to
at threshold, ply our trades for shelter
on earth, poetry in interstices, totally, lie thee down
                                        to rise

Anne Waldman
Juneteenth 2021

Dear Hassan,

The tremor of hills: resistance
The toxicity of orange: fierce
The arrangement of metal: precise
The biodegradability of us: mortal
The casting of manners: loud
The sustainability of affection: strong
The encounter of trains: crossed
The quirk of knowing: told
The corporeality of skin: irreplaceable
The quickness of purchase: here
The creation of loss: historical
The nerve of thought: red
The fort of building: character
The sweat of google: screened
The hollow of horizon: dug
The surrender of nothing: humanoid
The lip of delivery: landslide
The time of ending: capitalism
The question of being: yes
The gold of armour: something
The freeze of feeling: determined
The melancholy of fill: there
The solution of green: today

October 14

Dear Jérémy Robert,

The light turned in facets and I am in
Cincinnati at the BLINK festival, having just
read Simone White's *Unrest* and an interview
with Layli Long Soldier, and corresponding
with you about Etel Adnan's plays
and I am thinking about how lovely these
individuals are including yourself, and what
a road to find them, and thinking too about
the painstaking words (I meant to say
"work"), and trying to reach the body of
language or the bodies in language, and
how Julia Carlson uttered those
words coming out of an elevator, and I
was immediately drawn to her. For there
are bodies in the words, massacres in
them, massacres in the documents
the treaties, the owning, the ownership
the books. Is it language that can bring
down language, or bodies bring down statues?
Can Columbus Day be renamed Indigenous
People's Day? An upheaval of thought. What
does it mean to rename?

Love,
Sarah

Jérémy's reply:

May 5

Dear Sarah,

what does it mean to rename? to race
rainbows hush-rushing to the ocean when
light pink milk & knocked-out blue ping
pong over the cloud-clad sky to catch
a cold in red-hot rain and say they maim
and say our names to take shame down
and build words up to shape a world in
but one word a few have heard a bird
its fate owning not owing and see anew

Love,
J.

Dear Lyric Hunter,

      The hand ran away with the hour
and the hour came back with a vengeance
nothing personal. The bee was so very
large and we were watching it
peering into its busy-as-a-something
a creature which we were too
the insects milling about minding their
own business, and we humans getting
involved, very curious, determined to
know, to manipulate, to shift, to alter.
Yet there is you finding a place in
the world, finding a dress in the world
a peace, a way to be, around singing
and exchanging, bookselling, leaning in
toward books and the fan fiction
listening, eating rice and beans, smiling
learning some words of Scottish, adoring
the chipmunks and the butterflies, or were
they moths, and the very soft looking
Mexican pine. Somehow the feeling is good
between us, and we revel, emerging
out of systems, bigger than they
or so much smaller, and we smile and
our eyes meet and we are happy for a moment.

Kathleen Fraser:

        The lane it was fickle and the
amoeba syllables waltzing this way and
that a torrential fire and smoke so thick
my nephew can't go to school and we in an
underpass waiting for a moment, that moment
and the screens proliferating and the tracing
of De Kooning's hand, your mother's, your hand
and it came along lonely for the gesture
and she had alzhiemers, you not returning
e-mails, deflecting to your publisher
or else asking for written correspondence
with postage stamps, and me writing
this letter, loving you, remembering you
in Rome, in Paris, in San Francisco
smiling, suspending, that huge smile
living there in that, talking over
the melon and the prosciutto, HOW 2
your work translated for a Double Change
reading at the galerie éof, by Omar and
Abigail, projected, the stuttering
syllables, determined flights of mind
something in the foreign and we and
you, and you and you and you

August

O.,

The light it was this way and if you
walked across it, laughing, in deep knowledge
of all that was happening in Barcelona, the
light would shift a little and come into
our eyes and cause us to squint a bit
aligned as you are with the sun
and you reach your hand out still laughing
as the freedoms are restricted and the
bodies are falling. What one could I
love more than you as we wade through
the rising waters and the winds and
weather, nature angry with us
and you selected "randomly" for
an extra search on the plank up
to the airplane and me there crying
my face turned away from the children
who are playing even then and I refusing
to move forward. Any one of us could be taken
away from the others in a second. I felt that
as I picked up a dove outside our window
its flight likely halted by our glass.
The second doesn't care
any more than the weather

To Uljana,

The draft of wade is air.
The current of red is darned.
The circle of familiar is electric.
The summonings of tail is flap.
The remainder of ethos is branching.
The breath of telling is zip.
The coast of returned is zealous.
The quirk of azalea is patch.
The muscle of fortune is flip.
The shock of trickling is shade.
The quarter of how is texture.
The century of land is removed.
The articulation of zero is something.
The Anna of approval is it.
The marked of seldom is such.
The grazing of nose is O.

10/23/17

Dear James,

       There was along a cradle finishing the
knot something born that would know doom
but what was not already known into
that jar or melody some quickening and
that hollow an echo in here inside the belly
of a whale with my father and already having
a long nose the weight of western civilization
leaning on a lie and progress and development
meaning their opposites and she looked into that
dictionary for the word "dear" and found there
no direct equivalent, no term of endearment
and address separated out from the people
the feeling attached to: grandmother
father, beloved, sister
brother, mother and so on. Did you
look for the animal, the deer, Elyce asked
saying that so many of our poses in yoga
come from animals, and if not from
animals, from myths? Then she recalled
the line in one of the many books Omar is
accumulating on racism and slavery, that racism is a
form of making meaning. Books make
meaning but books are not all good.
I wonder what you would say to that

Fall

Dear Donna,

     It came in with the sun and
your life a film without an ending
wrapping around the clouds and
buildings, forming architecture
of tender provision and fresh awakening
tossing open the words to empathy
and comprehension. We tight
along that indeterminate, letting in
room for breath, so too the dampening
a way to let slide, further along
with the light some yellow strands
who to quicken the never—quite—
random nature of time and event
close very how, and the way the weight of it
the colors of it, remembering how
and making way for the it of it

          Sarah

All Souls' Day

Geneva,

      The cat struck two and immeasurably
in that interval, pain, and determining the
fierce shade of orange, we too walk into that
place, along a meteor steadily coherent
arranging the green, some more ploughed over
and it is kin to the mouse, to tell the
undercurrents and how deceived, more
quickly along a sputtering that change
into a green curve and there lover retrieved
made step

        how too such further knotted
tied ring, for the anomaly of deranged time
spread sidewalk horror in there every slight
and yet your smile tricked in the night
turned furiously toward allay should
border made troubled cacophony coming out
and there your kids all souls tremendous
you that exceeding brave veering a
rendered craze, caught, spinning out
and we, thought so and so, forever
line warped around and telling

      in that there, thirst memory
walk and a wall

January

Dear Karla Kelsey,

Sea to the vote: is planted
Braid along lines: ways of tumult
Fast the angle: in a green kaleidoscope
Harbor the prairies: flash inward
Amusing vein: calling to determine
Further to cat: spread the griffes
Remember the surface: a rattled sort of spit
Taken with incline: a grass soul
Figured in zero: a molten length
Followed nerve: thought to the basin
Iridescent word: you chew syllables
Eight to the album of we: easing into terror

Dear Norma,

      It was relaxing to take out words and
gather energy around drawing—you knew
it, and we were painting our hair white—
the very strokes of it—along a kindred
spirited yay-saying, and the flesh tones the
hardest part but there would be colors
many many colors.

Dear Gia,

Gather the energies you have spread out,
                     said Elyce.

Perhaps now is the time, you said,
                     to accept.

Just the word, written in an e-mail,
                     death.

Let them cry here, on the leaves
                     of cut trees.

I watched the dancers in Alvin Ailey
                     give their all.

Here is our being, says Rachel: what it needs,
          where it hurts, which gifts it has to offer.

Dear Julie,

The delay is a feature and the hour
is quiet. We fell through a hole and found
a small maze leading to a bigger one.
So to train of thought coming round the
mountains. It delivers and the gifts
are torn at the seams. We looked at each
other and smiled for a long time. How
could I come back, how could I not.
Frames of arrival and one girl's very deep
voice carrying over a crowd. You said
it was for the girls and so we lift
off in adventure. Always this balancing
between new experience and routine.
Here is where capitalism meets fascism. We
are sad, disempowered. If
you look at the work of Sonia Delaunay
before the war came, and then it
dies off. Wondering alternatives

Love,

Sarah

Julie Patton's reply:

I am grateful for this tender spell link, feel warm, excited and privileged to hear from you....

I read this yesterday with much hope in reverence for I couldn't summon the right words to respond ... so wrapped up in its song, meanings wings taking me all over the place your mind went before.... Meanings, also for what English can and can't hold—another syntax ... seams between the spaces, blade....

voice carrying over ... indeed ... part of what I might read to my sister today when I go to light a candle by her grave, 30 years gone ... AIDS.... And her husband, an out gay man who thought marriage would spare his life, all wrapped up in hers, it shook then took....

Then there is Amanda Gorman's voice—speech, oration still carrying the crowd. She, her presence and poise perhaps even more the poem and the Poem-being. Canary gold in the goal mind.... Hopefully less and less *where capitalism meets fascism* in celebrity-excess with its all or nothing, here or be damned exploitive rings. I hope it does something wise for poetry *can* offer much wisdom for a deaf and dumb culture. Some of the words, pauses and gestures of the inauguration did feel like a much needed release. Even a healing for I already feel lighter, and more hopeful. And sunnier. When Amanda pronounced the word *light* the sun did come out. But only for a minute before it slipped right back into its NE Ohio leaden bloom. And wisps of snow. I wasn't the only one amazed by this. Poet Tony Medina mentioned it. But here in Ohio, it was truly something to see because the sun had been absent for all but 1.5 days out of 30. A grave for a sky. But here we are ... alive and letting the word *poetry* work the crowd. Of course more mediocrity will step forward and be crowned.... We'll make do with mere elevated speech and a poem reciting president is definitely a see change. I can't even imagine what the response would be had the public heard poets ring words like yours.... But I can imagine it. Just as there's a Bernie mitten meme.... Amanda, with people putting words from other poems in her mouth ... might just carry forth, get people to look up and pay attention ... for youth itself is promise (and black so beautiful).... The world knows it. Tries to deny it. All peoples (independent of species) have that look in their eyes.... When the guns are lowered and replaced with song. When the clouds take a hike and....

Love,
Julie

Brooklyn Studio

Oh Tracy,

The math of the tell is addition.
To scan on the heart is blue.
The more of brace is grief.
To stage the period is undoing.
Attempting to be is being.
The sliding of thoughts is thought.
To tell the emoticons is emotion.
The reading of the branches is winter.
The sawing into soul is conditioning.
To move to exchange breaths.
The remainder of the season is what not.
Along a sight of existence: are.
Being together is a color and that color is.

Tracy Grinnell's response:

dearest Sarah,

> to sleep   and die   I was an hour
> in any other dream   I was
> an hour of a thousand children   an
> hour illuminated by rage   I
> was an hour that held a burning branch
> an hour   I was
> an hour that was   breach
> with two   iron lungs   I was
> an hour   of loss
> of the violence of broken   arms I
> was an hour that went numb in the face
> of someone   an hour   between
> two points of departure   an hour
> that never returned   I   was
> an hour   in the abyss   the mouth of
> an hour   held   the image   of a
> dream   an hour the night returned   an hour
> where no sound   escaped   my mouth
> I   was   an   hour   away   I   was
> an unclaimed   hour   a wandering   ghost for an
> hour   I was all   it was   to hold   a shape
> around a space   an hour   composed of
> many hours   I was an hour   each night   that
> was left to die   in dreams that   formed
> each day   before   an hour   I was resolved
> to form   a figure   in parts   an hour   of glass

18june2021

Dear Susan Bee,

      There was a tackling of sunsets and
your job was to keep going, the darker the
time the more colorful the paintings.
It was a series of connections, the
big rally against the new tax bill.
You said you both had to keep going—
others said how well you were doing—
that you had to for the sake of your
living child. The chocolate was from
America you said, and that no one ever serves
chocolate from America. There was a lot
of speaking and not many chances
to speak, and it made me think ironically
of Charles' title *Close Listening*, and
later how artists are misfits in some
ways and the art helps counterbalance.
Not a new thought, not an original thought
but a thought felt differently. And
me reading a book on twenty ways to
live, and the first one being not
to be afraid of death because—get this,
it feels good.

Casablanca

Dear Karen,

The accrued range is a melancholy yes
though the strips of thought are grilled on each side
to the tower of our upheavals myriad fingerprint
coming alongside the palm of your hand
pain is in that eyebeam but told in syllables if that
we could manage each display as fraught
so even what you had to say, maternal
a matrix of conundrum and befuddlement
wanting to call you again and lay it out
there in our hands some children and the knowledge
of having voted, of turning over in our beds
some kind of vexation that is head to
impeachment, would be nice, but we
can't fool ourselves about the fearsomeness
of this moment—Safira cut her finger
almost invisibly so, but that you asked
if her mother kissed it, led to action, action
a kiss, and that is what we have and
it is power also into the fingers, the brains
turn over intuition and you have it on our sleeves

Letter poem from Souad Labbize:

Dear Sarah,

Words in lockdown
stay hung
on the laundry line
as long as the sun
doesn't receive a visa
on its travel document
Your letters to dear ones
are the many seasons
of a language to come

Dear Souad,

      An empire of trances
whispers in the secret zooms.
We have met but far away.
The rim of your glasses red-orange
round. You are holding the
words, not letting them go,
they are round and rimmed orange
smiling slyly, mouths
or something. You wrote
me first, and I, seeing
your poem on a laundry line
strung from an albizia tree. Stamens
fall with the visas, a shower
of red lines, how to pronounce
the cantilever of connection.
Sabrina wrote revolution backwards
and it had love in it. Sending
you that there, Souad, in the letters,
circling backwards, or around

Dear Zahra,

The sand of removal from thinking
sidestepping toward that branch leaning this way
and that, a garden in the middle of the city.
Some kids, your students, thinking on things
the melting of progress so that it's not
a capacity for reaching and if staying in place
the fraught considerations honored there.
Some relaxing, a dozen other thoughts,
some dozen thoughts relaxing.
Then Safira turns and says: if this were
the time of slavery would I be black or white?
Questions with a thousand answers
and I find one: not precisely knowing
explaining the 1/8th rule, the "why is that?"
crestfallen look on the face of a 9-year-old,
not mentioning yet this a time of
slavery, that it continues: finding the ways
through, working with language. Zahra, oh wow.

Savannah,

The snow in the air is damaged.
Your hair is purply weeping.
We raised an empty glass to her soul.
Sinking to the lake bottom with your voice.
Handling the sky with marks.
Laughing into a container said news.
Every day a march in the heart ventricles.
You are soothing the earth with your tails.
She whisked the edges just so.
A container marked balloons & sticks.
So to the future, a compendium
of human foibles, love daggers
so, so sorry.

O.,

The brittle of ease: those branches
A taint of row: this place
Followed in steps: a single torrent
Place name divider: intermittent light
And to the left ear: a remainder
Following the sound: along arms
And to the two of it: a quadrupling
Right in the light: some backs approaching
Solemnly misfit: a harrow of film
To the left again: a silk of endings
Approaching the main: rhythms arriving
Tossed and joined: some mirroring
And the locus of difference: in there
We in a place: the clustering
Mottled and arranged: sequence be

Overcast

Dear Laynie,

The share of the moment into rain
Dropping wholly fallow into winter
Same nest to the endangered minute
Instance of credulity in the ochre earth
Partaking in the grasses including sorrow
Example of colors warn into barrels
More to the rending futures a detail
If wracked in planetary gossip
Less the tremendous fill not to find
A parsing of skin to be dangerous
The making of texture that place
Or forgoing a grip to the spacing

Laynie's reply:

Dear Sarah,

Rain of dictionaries names
Winter atelier of sinuous lines
Minutes twine and eyes are made
Earth—of gold ink—over-dipped
Sorrow includes soft sounds bursting
Barrels, engines of credulity, an upward
Detail of deeply notched leaves and mended flowers
Gossip is also planetary matter
Fine nests of leaflets and nettles
Dangerous unless approached with attention
Place fingers to stem
Spacing tremulous futures
Cast embossed text into rings

Love,
Laynie

Dearest Franck and Françoise,

Mystery and containment: a song
The pandemic steps: like Sisyphus
A batch of learning: getting up there
Gouache New York and Frida: the runner ducks!
An uninhabitable annex: breathing
Bending with traditions: calling to prayer
Friendship in a necklace: moment on the phone
                              from the 19th arrondissement
Frailty woven together: a batch of understanding
Bordeaux one of the slave ports: x-spot denial
Sending you SOS: you responding still
A series of letters this time: consuming poems with wine

Dear Damon,

The chart of the hereafter caught in the stairs
A remembered dialogue between three people figured
to the poles
So as a reminder of ash conversation burning
The retreat into words riding through them
Burning of the knight brigade some codes of honor
Reevaluating the centuries for the present leaning into it
And the next ones caught in clouds
A message to incense there a digging
Shall through tipping way: earth equilibrium
Impossible to have it back: what we take for granted
And a soul or two: rushing back
Certain removal: caught in
But you say it: regeneration

Geneva:

To the succor of plants on not an island
Some mixing with the consonants boldly
into planning along a design of tribute
barely telling Ching-In Chen said immigration
and the word comes at angles and
indentations: experience through a mesh
of harassment and infringement, no language
that could be extricated, the pronouns
they and their hard won, the cutting
up the page not some free act: a
way of surviving, what it takes
for me to realize this, a lot
the Kelsey St. book closes and the
world is there, changing

Geneva Chao's response:

a lesson in letters and their position
which is meaning in company or null in
isolation refracted in solitude the moment of
heart bursts forth in a wish of flourish
in a refusal of notoriety in an entreaty for
understanding no public no frog no tendrils and gentle
hooks thrown out for context for *situation* no
comfortable seats no entourage

only the imagined sea & the knowledge that all of your
names
will desert you & I will cradle the petal that's left

Dear Safira,

The rest of the world (is not) resting.
The thing I wanted to say is telling.
The whole of the half I whole in you.
Such is the gasp for breath and then breathing.
The sucking to find succor you are.
We went to the pharmacy to find cream.
Your hair a mane over your ukulele.
The song is the words you find.
The place is the house of love for you.
The world is crying and you know it.
Your smile cures ailments.
Your eyes accompany the terrible.
You just you together with us.
The oceans of the world are spreading.
The plastic is choking the sea turtles.
The color of skin is not blind.
You can see and you sing.

Evening

Dear Janice,

The fusing of voice with voice: awesomely simple
A category hurricane in the eye: the stranger
We in friendship along syllables: demanding
Strength in gathering: a left to the birds
Frontal the attacks: you to the uttering
Wisdom in diagonals: tweetering
A hand to keyboard: knowing being
Guts in out: showing up with music
Making of the instant: what becomes love
This is what we can do: ripe for harmony
And the angling: be, to be with intention

Dear Alystyre,

Thoughts curled up in your eyes
and some ideas of other
& sameness came out in Arabic
a bird preening itself during the rain
of Darwish's poem and your eye shifting
here document—we do this, we do that
accompanied by cascades of affection
the woman-daughter director steps on stage
Rebecca Miller is her name and she tells us
of her epiphany to become a filmmaker
clusters of friends eating bagels and all
she had to do was buy the bagels
and her mother the famous photographer
cooked for them: the films came like poems
through the window onto the kitchen sink
and we caught each others' smiles
and laughed for a while, each
day a new day, and each minute
passing through your hand on, be

Alystyre Julian's response:

Dear Sarah,

Thoughts curl up in these letters
Each moment streams through your ears
Each letter a new letter
Impressed upon your wild irises
A new quiet settles between
Africa and Alaska-six letters
Arabic sunrise and Tlingit sundown
We do this-we do that-document in iris light
A daughter does her dives; a Mountain changes face
Meaningful material
An eagle's nest, top of tree, triangular, viewed without
binoculars
The Eagle has its inlet
Pink salmon on the run, their restless gills end up in trees
We smile on the bridge
Cascades of affection
Come like poems through the kitchen window onto the
kitchen sink
Bouquet of flame
Gush of wilderness, be

Clarinda Mac Low:

Tales of meager replies and gasp sky
thoroughly taken on a platform feet to
quickening detail along a force to held
Merely conniving out of in tell palm
Woman warrior skipping over wood
Even to wilting a strong sensation there too
No melancholy in that will to move
Some torrents quill or arch back
A definite tiptoe frozen along veins
Or nearing that contention flip back
without remorse some wonder along lines
a quavering rippling of tales and onto
slapping no some pivoting under shrinking
vacillating electric energy through to floor
how the remainder suckles under
knees and joints alive and kicking
waving to the mystery or finding the air
a hip thing not exactly wriggling
and you too in the remembrance of bends
furrowing and fiddling in a fierce way
back to the report of it nestling

Dear Aya,

The coronation of the minute
We in a gesture held
Two traces of shadow and some
       temperate thoughts
Formerly mellow reaching in there
Quarry of worries raised thoughtfully
Further back: you walking on
       a sidewalk in a country where
           you've never been
Some arrangements returned and
       provocative
Surrounding the time with gossamer
Healing growing roots between us
A smile stretched to the edges
       of the world
Wherever that might be

March 9

Dear Aya Nabih,

So the eyes open: along a line to there
Some more tremendous times: in the blue
The arch of an arm: more to the picture
Sorely so to the fall: leaves by the old barn
And to the process: trying out different animals
The long journey from the airport: cooking together
We were apart by a few feet: then inches
Eyes open and waiting: being
And to that you bring: presence
The constraints of the everyday: wrapped around
Our eyes meeting: in mutual blindness
To trust in that: and to gesture

April 2, 2018

Dear Meg,

The utter minute has arrived: we are here
There are some thoughts: over to you
The syncopated sounds of the bassist: a woman!
We are women in intersecting cultures
If you come off as bad or bad-ass it makes sense
The rules are different: and you are different from
the rules
What was it about the rules again? Which ones
Laughing over imagining your mother on FB
The writing on the wall given a different tilt
We are in a basement: this is the U.S.
You know Tanzania: nothing in Black Panther is it
Nothing is it: but for your assured lines
Cascading over your you-ness

April 3

Dear Celina Su,

The kick would come: almost a cup, or a cup
Twenty robins in a field: one oriole in a tree
Heard you at McNally: some signs of poetry
Or is it spring: or winter
Life stirs and you are smiling: maybe Taiwanese
citizenship
A sonogram in Morocco: a book with Belladonna
Enjoying the matzo ball soup: this café I know from
the outside
Movies set there: and we in
This field stretched before you: a four-floor walk up
The smile comes back: we are becoming friends
Same day magnolia and Hiroshige snowed branches
Some meetings at the U.N.: talk of teaching and health
care

Celina's reply:

February 2, 2021

Dearest Sarah,

Between the lines of your poem, a gift. I recall that hyper-ventilating taxi ride through the outskirts of Fez, as if she had been born by caesurae.

This morning, the aforementioned kick spies a steel water tower on a building across the street, declares affection for the robot. The crunch of her boots sinking into the crème brûlée of one-day-old snow.

In my mind's eye, the rhythms of lap swimming at the Y under fluorescent lights, your ink line drawings projected behind you in the second-floor manuscripts room of the public library, the sensation of the escalator en route. Almost moving away for a year, to be with a grandmother, and in the meantime, the oud, in the meantime, fleeing Los Angeles to rescue a language.

This year of purgatory is crowned *unprecedented*, but no pigs fly outside my window. So I attempt to interrogate exactly which logics are now suspended, and how many simply slip on cloaks of invisibility.

On blankets shared on the north end of the park lawn, in galleries accompanied by the whooshing of Yan's balloons filling with air, of Elena's sewing machine threading palin-dromes across generations and continents. This afternoon, she points to the rooster felt doll, or as she calls it, the chicken with a heart-shaped hat.

For Lunar New Year, my father's girlfriend gives my daughter a red envelope with a $100 bill. I am not allowed to refuse it, even though she just gave a two-year-old more than a day's wages. She has been on the waiting list for Section 8 housing vouchers for more than a decade. A grammar of survival, a syntax of lagniappe.

I think of her subway commute. Ensconced in our respective homes, grappling in this longest month for the semblance of a pattern of grief, a sentence becomes a kind of privilege. Research as devotion.

I long for conspicuous absence, this presence of willful abstention in our onion-skinned histories of the immediate, resistance to the seduction of despair. In our virtual real rectangles with you, Mirene and I hopscotch, motherless mothers without mother tongues.

Our memory palaces packed with many-digit inflation rates and annotations of South American semi-precious stones, with impossible knots of material belonging, perhaps with *oxalá*, as my childhood neighbors would say. Each time, I think of Candomblé.

Tonight, we turn off our table lamps. When we hear a whirring sound, the toddler announces, *It's not a star. It's an airplane.* The night sky fills the bedroom with a bright pink, snow reflecting. This, too, is winter.

You write, *a snow shower of poems.* Make room for. Coffee, email, podcast, zoom accordions of your work. Each gesture a correspondence, each paragraph an attunement, a community in the whispers of our various lullabies, names like pronouns, relational rather than absolute.

If what belongs to you is *yours*, what belongs to me is *mines*.

Dear Vincent Broqua,

Land-locked and derived, a mellow compartment
There to the something avenue poised on an artichoke,
or two
Severed and delivered, rolling speech
Quickly in the wonder, staccato
A performance solo into mane
Frightening there tremulous
You laughed to determine whereabouts
As the center of souls
There to the steps leading up and down
Tracie Morris wow-ing Albertine
And you to the angle articulate
So more or less uttered, you are singing
You in flight, landing here and there

April 20

Dear Eléna Rivera,

The sensation of loss is tremor
The season of temporality is liquid
The query into analogue is thorough
The mixture of window is late
The hollow of disaster is repeating
The tossing of angle is align
The wisdom of temptation is filling
The quick of lingering is that
The detox of mind is spirit
The calendar of quickness is alert
The meander of joy is spotted
The telling of sugar is a laugh
The welling of hearing is whisper
The quake of body is present

Eléna's reply:

Dear Sarah,

Will we ever recover flocks of loss
The following year breaks hands
The question of being divides me
& wind's duration causes a squall
Large crusts form over ancient history
Our hearts vibrate harder, packed
my fingers keep stroking the border
My stomach responds to agreement
Emptiness embodies the framework
& warm hands rub a new configuration
Will I let myself rejoice day & night
Let's not forget winter's appeal, its call
as I take my place in turbulent echoes,
in the murmuration of a physical body

Dear Self,

The drift and yes to the committee
Not just to the left and right: all the directions
To color, to substance, to equality
Incorporating all, nothing
Relinquishing, fluctuating
We along design, realizing, telling
Flung, embrace, quality
Handsome, landslide, that work
Fear, something, the 10-year-old girl
        you were, always also are
Freedom, from tertiary, into the multiple
        co-existence, always

May 4

Dear One,

The change into birds and a draft
       in the atmosphere
The lanes dividing and deteriorating
       off at an angle
Wished for the privacy of a hollow
       departure
And then returning into mellow
       mere thought
Some temperature at ease in the
       blending
Friday into shortening minutes
Telling time to give in such determinacy
The wake of a thread
       around tunnels
And a dashing into rain
       heated movement
But for the angle of casing
       meandering hip

To Donna,

The tracing of those heels in layers of cement
Wandering in a city carrying out how
Along the lines of remove and determine
Frighteningly so peoples' lives in there
Some remainder only dense telling in roots
Thickly coming in a revisiting of place
To whisper or gasp: also in or along
Folding upwards only shelves of energy
The tossing of the co-signatures
Frowned upon and the merits of the
Trees communicating with each other
Between cities only in one place

Dear Lyric,

The venture into train: a misstep
It did happen: now to find balms for the heart
A rendering lake: arrival at a shrine
Mood aria: where withal within
She spooked the meter: and a degree toward fahrenheit
Landing at a moving vehicle: mere telling
There to produce definitions: sorrow renditions
Droning as bee: spread out among a relationship
Farther held out: the practice of plants
And the harrowing return of the pretty jay: thing
Remarked to also motion: we enough
Queried into remainder: solemnly yes
Spurts of joy at the rhododendron: here

May 12, 2018

Dear Reader,

I had heard from you lately
and the news is complex

Dear Reader,

I had meant to tell you
Look behind the gate.
Can you fetch that package?
It is for you
Please open it up when you
        get the chance
There are leaves in there
        layer upon layer of them
They are a bit wrinkled, in stacks
Can you remove the plastic
        that crept in there
My great aunt's family received
        a bomb in its mailbox
Invitation or at least incentive
        to leave
Which packages do we get
        and send?

Dear Etel,

Those thoughts circle back
We had heard through the ocean
The creatures in troubled waters
We creatures turning about
Merely muse and a wonder
For the cavity. In there a coffee
Running alongside some questions
And you answered in green
You always answer in colors
The torrential thoughts in a window
or a cloud

Dear Karla,

The venture of the frost was nourished
The cancelling of remember was late
The tissue of the plant forgiveness
The tears of the red raccoons a pond
The quickening of the ending sky apparent
The orange of the caliber tremendous
The removal of tempests not plausible
The delay of the fury and interdiction
The query into blossom multi-furcated
The slender quaver of harmony told
Some rush into birdseed suspended
The certainty of memory to remove
Anger about weapons that maim
Healing a possibility only gray matter
And in the solitude of one stick a breathing
Such quintessential furthering of the mane

May 27, morning

Dear Rachel,

The leviathan woke up casually next
                    to my right arm
We were sisters or brothers, this thing
                    and I
Some, most, didn't see it, the species dying off
It was like blinking an eye, or two
Then they were gone—we too
How was it we were still writing
                    each other
Like an afterlife of sorts
The most we ever did
I wrote on paper
My 84-year-old father told me
          I was obsolete in a lot of ways
Even stringing together whole sentences
A coup
Thought we love each other and somehow
          this is never obsolete

Rachel's reply:

April 30, 2021

Dear Sarah,
Yes. To coup
to many Coups
Naying.   May
a joyous spot find you –
Sarah, I believe in souls.

In you, fate or person
correct or incorrect
Notion   Karma –
that we come, that
          we come in with it –
Coup.   This

Leviathan, upon which
today   I harm.
Insane   Coup –
floated metal
a forever cup for
water or   whatsoever

emptiness   &
below over to the
Left   city double
(2 manhattans please)
barreling waste from
They say

Way
before we knew -
               how do we –
know now?   how to teach

these,   our newstellers
Telling us How –

Why   slather byproducts
how, why, name, tell,
scratch an itch
for escape   Tell our children
they aren't   their things aren't
quite right

Dear Emily Johnson,

Further into the concrete your dog's eyes
A reminder of the layers of water and history
Your face a cinema of emotions
To give back to the East River
The water it had given, the something
A silent walk from Danspace, St. Marks
There were a dozen, maybe fifteen of us
All coming from somewhere
Speaking of the somewhere from which they came
Your words inaudible with all the traffic
And yet I could hear your meanings
Climbing over the wall to the rocky bank
Of the river for you to return the water
And then for us to gather garbage
Washed up on the shore
A collective act, a grimace, a smile

Late Evening

Dear You,

The remainder of the hullabaloo was catching
More were catching in each second
Some left on the table, only hour only twine
So to the purpose of a remaking
Quick enjoinders and a laugh
Solemn enclave roaring throughout
Merely catching stars you said
Along a dash toward nothing, in it
Lengthy rejoinders, that was correct
Or nearly, everything nearly,
A dime a dozen, the plants imperiled
We along an ocean, along a planet

Later

Dear You,

The toss of the turvy and twist
Some sibilance slopped into shape
Rear reformers in the rental raked
Must movers merely mistaken
Not nefarious with nipples nought
Or officiating ospreys over and out
Pests and peepers pale to pipers
Queer queen question queue
Under or upon utterly useless but unique
Velvet and veneer voluptuous veering
Who what where when westerly

May 31, 2018

Dear You-as-They,

What to the now of the equation
Equally toned to the removal and
       Freed from constraints
Blistered and remaindered
People peeling back that effigy
Forgiving to the maximum
Undertone and relaxed
So too the terror flabbergasted
Some melancholy in that ear
The release of total strangers
Furthermore a reminder
In that kinship and success
Reeling in answers, strains of
          melody
You too to the wonder in pain

June 4

Dear Reader,

I had erased the part where
        we talked
Some former ways of going mad
You too were determined it seemed
        not to understand
But you were still reading, your
        eyebrows crossed
It was a way of conversing anyhow
        without tongues
And in that angle an exchange
        of eyes
What color are yours?
In the waking definition of tremendous
Somewhere creased and taking
Laughter in that pupil, joy
For to the furthertime run down
And some answers fully clothed

Laynie:

Quirk in the spectrum of how
No thing unturned or swallowed
The surrendered curriculum of fish
Mournfully pre-dated and tweeted
Framework of an absent under arm
We had understood shriveled seconds
and kindnesses forlorn angled
So to the twirl of the conch thrown
Formerly caught in the brain
Or star at the train spun
Into sibilance a fragrant shot
Without legs and the torn tears
We wished for vanished t's
A chance toward breaking
Three streams in a silt pavement

Dear Emily Wallis Hughes,

The surrounds of attention focalized in a rose
Methodically to the wherewithal some peace
And on their minds were famines
caused by colonies and everything caused by colonies
yes also the weather—we sat in a garden
for a time we didn't count. The gardens
built through colonies. The pansies looking at us.
Some deteriorating lines. And in that angle
several eyes detached and circling.
The politics of flowers. They too in the flight
path. The fight path. The fight song.
Examining the difference between collective
and collaborative. Daffodils and daisies.
Who lives and who doesn't and how.

August 11

Dear Elodie,

The scent of deliberation is turned
The quick of soul is thick
The mayor of time is floating
The day of your day is Tetouan
The who of the admiration is kind
The mirror of thought is original
The peach of gift is taken
The fortitude of summer is coming
The red of the assurance is soft
The answer of fourth is a branch
The remainder of cicadas is soon

Bettina,

I met you under your hat
and you took my hand and
held it there the recognition
of time and space that I know
from others—Etel, Babia—after
90 somehow

Then in another moment
from over your wheelchair
came that hand again
this time with a card you said:
of mother and child

Here is one shape
with many dimensions: if there
are individuals tilting this way
and that, they are enveloped,
balanced, a bit as a mobile,
perhaps even set sail without a sky
or sea necessary

Elegy for my Uncle

The sound of the hour is blue
The lake of reflection is starry
The pen of the heart is itself
The change of the sky is here
The memory of the swings remains
The telling of the encounter is forever
The boxes of making are indigo
The form of the mind is this
The gift of the self is keen
The clock of the pause is heard
The blink of the butterfly is present
The sun of the shine is passing
The subways of imagination are love
The moon of the breeze is flutter
The smile of remembrance is you

To Basel

The rain on your hair inside
winnowed its way into cell
phones and alarms quietly I
wrote on your hand your beautiful
mind cannot be contained try
as they might it was wonderful
to see you in the dream we were
laughing in an arrangement
of hours talking to the melt
heartbreak and deliberate
strength a mellowing of talking
for so many just a being

Dear Yto,

The tail of the land: a place
A remainder in telling: formidable
Some flies to the left: a promise
A forlorn avenue: let in
Surreptitiously delivered: horizon
When to the rain: furthermore
An arrangement in time: so
Moreorless certain: arrivals on flowers
Mating in the avenue: telepathy
Strange and pearl: those eyes
Mixed and more: a plate handed over
Telling the question: you to answer
A quarrel hovers: in the second
And a name: so sure, forever
The last one being: someone else's beginning

Dear Pete,

Lately the loss in avalanche
And back then, and further back too
We had queried the choir, organized
               the incense
Something came at angles anyhow
Fortunately hollow some day
We and a wish and a place
The fall comes holding the bird seed
Wondering about the stove
Myriad the shapes of tears
And your brother needing you now
               until the end
The end of life: what is it
The light diagonal, the tops of trees
Turning in a forest, these words
Holding us together, not to feel alone